CLAIRVOYANT:
My Definition
My Story

[klɛr'vɔɪənt] → 声称能够预见未来的人. 先知.
definɪʃən → 清晰度. 必然.

by Marcus Howell
['markəs]
马库斯 豪厄尔

The characters and events in the book are fictitious. Any similarity to real persons, living or dead, is coincidental, and not intended by author.

Copyright © 2013 by Marcus Howell

All right reserved. In accordance with the U.S. Copyright Act of 1976, the scanning, uploading, and electronic sharing of any part of the book without the permission of the publisher is unlawful piracy and theft of the author's intellectual property. Thank you for your support of the author's rights.

Haiku

Judge not what is not understood, instead try to educate yourself

~Soltreu~

Clairvoyance

Today, in my mind, I stood alone
at the edge of the universe
and looked into the infinite, wordless wisdom -

Coming back
towards earth, always
awed by its colors
this gift hung by God in the night sky
about the size of my hand -
glad to call it home from this distance.

Closer, more cluttered
now the creatures of earth
the buildings and the roads
and compassion replaces awe -

I wish to fill the universe with
this compassion and bring the clarity

from the edge of the universe
But I cannot.

In the garden, so much lost -
until I look into the face of the first spring flower.

by Laurie Conrad

FOREWORD
By Soltreu

At thirty-seven years old, I have known *Markie* (his childhood nickname) since I was nineteen. He has always been like an older brother to me. His genuine care and concern for me has carried me through many hardships. I moved with Marcus for several months in November of 2008 until March 2009. This wonderful Being protected me my entire time in Georgia.

I always knew there was something special, in a supernatural way, about Marcus but never truly experienced it until he shared some things with me concerning my father. What I thought was going to be a tearful reading became a joyful reunion with my father who was murdered when I was five years old.

I initially, believed in Marcus' gift because I believed in him as a man of his word. Once I experienced first-hand the definition of his clairvoyance, I knew this GOD-given gift would help many people in many ways.

Marcus Howell has a gift. He uses it to change the world by helping people get closer to what GOD needs them to see. He is not trying to redefine what it is to be clairvoyant. Marcus wants to share his journey in order for others to better understand his gift and themselves. I ask that you open up, and allow GOD to move in you through Marcus. I know you will find out who you are even if it's just a little bit more than you already know. This is not rocket science. This is simply "***Clairvoyant: My Definition, My Story.***"

Table of Contents

Chapter 1) first signs

Chapter 2) waking up

Chapter 3) de ja vu

Chapter 4) daddy

Chapter 5) family gifts

Chapter 6) ok what's going on here?

Chapter 7) "psychic" class?

Chapter 8) professor x

Chapter 9) alcohol

Chapter 10) so much to do

Chapter 11) judging

Chapter 12) everyday clairvoyant

DEDICATED TO:

Three men who changed my life:

Charles Howell

Ulysses Cornell Walsh

Keith Nelson

And my three mothers who raised me to be the man I am today:

My mother,
Rosa Michelle Howell

My grandmother,
Natha Walsh

My God Mother,
Mrs. Christine Cook

INTRODUCTION

Clairvoyant is defined as being able to gain information and to see beyond natural abilities. It is a highly controversial gift in the psychic and paranormal genre often rejected by religious and secular realms.

Even parapsychological research is regarded as pseudoscience with a belief in the possibility of its existence being invalid due to over one hundred and thirty years of research. In short, skeptics believe, for clairvoyance to be true, it would be inexhaustibly clear by now.

In the NIV version of the Holy Bible, it states:

[1] Now about the gifts of the Spirit, brothers and sisters, I do not want you to be uninformed. [2] You know that when you were

pagans, somehow or other you were influenced and led astray to mute idols. ³ Therefore I want you to know that no one who is speaking by the Spirit of God says, "Jesus be cursed," and no one can say, "Jesus is Lord," except by the Holy Spirit.

⁴ There are different kinds of gifts, but the same Spirit distributes them. ⁵ There are different kinds of service, but the same Lord. ⁶ There are different kinds of working, but in all of them and in everyone it is the same God at work.

⁷ Now to each one the manifestation of the Spirit is given for the common good. ⁸ To one there is given through the Spirit a message of wisdom, to another a message of knowledge by means of the same Spirit, ⁹ to another faith by the same Spirit, to another gifts of healing by that one Spirit, ¹⁰ to another miraculous powers, to another prophecy, to another distinguishing between spirits, to another speaking in different kinds of tongues,[a] and to still another the interpretation of tongues.[b] ¹¹ All these are the work of one and the same Spirit, and he distributes them to each one, just as he determines.

This introduction is not a debate but a basis to understanding Marcus' hesitation about accepting what he now knows is a wonderful GOD ordained gift. This is simply his story about how he came to cultivate and use his clairvoyance. Now that this has been covered, let's get started.

But before we get started, you will notice many blank pages. These pages are for your notes. With each chapter, you will have questions and comments, so grab a pen or pencil for your journey through my story.

CHAPTER ONE: *First Signs*

Haiku:
In the beginning
There was GOD, and he knew things
HE passed IT to us
~Soltreu

As far back as I can remember; I was always a VERY imaginative child. Certain stories are still in my head as if they happened yesterday. Stories about Cherokee American Indians being in our family, and of my having a Cherokee name, *Wolves Ears*, are a few of them. I even heard members of my family had *certain* gifts as well. This discovery had me questioning *what* normal meant, and who *is* normal? Me? My family?

Everyone knew my grandmother, Natha, interpreted dreams, and one of my aunts could determine what detergent someone used in their clothes just from catching a whiff of them from any distance. She could even smell the phlegm in your body and instantly knew you had a cold. These memories became part of my guide through this journey of being Clairvoyant. But wait! I am probably losing you. Let me make it simple:

In the dictionary, clairvoyant is described as someone who is all seeing and can receive pictures or images in his or her mind beyond the norm. For my church folks, it is described as someone who has the gift of discernment. For example, some ministers or pastors are able to speak with someone or touch them and tell them about things going on in their lives without knowing them or their situation.

There are some people who want to discredit the gift by dirtying the word, psychic. There are also some who claim to have the gift with no proof of it. Because of this, I really dislike the word, psychic. It automatically puts the clairvoyant in a position to be made a joke without understanding what the gift truly is.

I now understand my gift and am comfortable with people knowing I am clairvoyant. My Faith in and love for GOD allows my gifts to grow stronger each day. He led me to this path making me a better man and child of HIS.

When I first heard the word, clairvoyant, I had no idea what it meant. It was about three years ago. I went home to Detroit to see my family *all because* my aunt who lives in London, Johnny Fiori, was in town. It was Super Bowl weekend 2009. I knew, for some strange reason, we were going to have a very educational and eye opening conversation.

That weekend became a serious turning point in my journey. That weekend answered many troubling concerns I had about myself growing up with this unknown gift. With my aunt, JJ, I felt we would end up having an all-telling moment.

Prior to the Super Bowl 2009 weekend, I discovered JJ on a few TV shows that aired here in

The States. It further confirmed I was on the right path. With JJ living in London, it is rare to catch her back home in Detroit. Watching one particular television show, *Most Haunted*, piqued my interest. My aunt was a special guest medium on the show who was invited to connect with spirits and energies at various haunted locations.

    Oh, let me backtrack. I often get ahead of myself. JJ has the clairvoyant gift as well, and in this visit back home, I wanted to learn more about it for validation of my gifts. OK, back to the show. This was a true shocker seeing her as a medium. Amongst all of her gifts including being a singer, an actress, and an all-around go-getter, I had no clue she was clairvoyant. It's quite ironic, because we have a lot of similarities almost like kindred spirits. I love to sing, and I have a very nice voice. I've done some acting before, even stage plays.

So, on that weekend, I went to JJ's mom's house where there was cooking, eating, drinking and just a festive family time, as we are known to have. As the festivities got started, in walked JJ, and out walked my nerves. LOL (laughing out loud).

I was beyond anxious about talking with JJ about her being a medium, and about what all of that meant. My deep dark anxiety ridden question was if I had that gift too.

Sometimes, we know the answers we seek but need validation, and in that same thought, we are nervous because what if we find out that which we are so sure about is not true? Devastating, right? Now, we are on the same page.

The opportunity soon presented itself for me to privately talk to JJ. As I fumbled with my wording, JJ burst out with this huge smile almost as if she was laughing inside. Her response to my inquiry was, "N*ephew, I believe that you are a 'TRUE CLAIRVOYANT*". At the time, I had NO clue what that meant, so I smiled and said thank you. LOL. She had some advice for my journey also, saying...

"Now baby, I want you to spend the next year learning what you're about to get into, because I want you to make sure you stay on the right path and learn how to ground and protect yourself and soak up any information you can. I want you to search the Internet, read some books, and find a class to learn about this gift."

I was initially excited and ready to learn, until I let stress cause me to question this gift. For the duration of that weekend, it was impossible to get any more alone time with JJ. I found that every time I had an opportunity she was being pulled in so many different directions by people who had not seen her in years. I did not want to seem selfish; I was just super excited about what she told me.

After singing, eating, dancing, and enjoying the rest of my weekend in Detroit, I figured I would catch JJ on Skype so we could converse more intimately about my path. With a six hour time difference, it was, of course, very hard to catch up with JJ. With work and everything else going on in my life, I finally promised myself I was going to have to figure much of this out on my own and not lean so much on JJ to hold my hand. That Super Bowl weekend in 2009, in JJ's mother's house, began my journey into the world of clairvoyance.

As my thoughts reached into my past about peculiar situations growing up, I later learned those were my first signs of being clairvoyant.

CHAPTER TWO: *waking up*

Cinquain Poetry:
Awake
No sleep
Once I'm aware
Nothing will shake it
Attentive
~Soltreu

Okay, so there's this weird feeling that comes over me whenever I talk with someone or have a reading. This started when I was in my early teens. It's difficult to explain, but I'm a firm believer that everything happens based off of energy.

Whenever I get a sudden chill or a blast of energy that would form around the top of my head, shoot down my neck through my shoulders, and continue down my arms straight through my feet, and back up towards my head, and radiate throughout my whole body, I knew it was starting.

Initially it felt good but as I have been developing my craft, it often feels a bit uncomfortable like a pain but not really a pain. The closest thing I can compare it to is when you are approached by the side vendors at the mall. They are always trying to sell you something, and in some stores, they have these hand or finger massagers that look like little metal hangers they rub over you. The vibration creates a tingling sensation around your head. That's the best way to explain that weird feeling I get whenever I do a reading; it catches you off guard. I learned that was the clairvoyance waking up. I had also learned in a class which is coming up later in another chapter that it's also a spiritual energy like what we call intuition that happens when your gifts are turning on.

    I think I was around 12 or 13 years old when I first felt this. It was during a long stretch in the morning, after waking up to get ready for school, when I felt this tingling sensation from the base of my neck. It exploded throughout my body causing me to enjoy the feeling. It felt relaxing like a back massage or like someone scratching my back and finding that spot I could never reach. It eventually became easier for me to generate my spiritual energy or intuition by simply wishing I could feel it again. In my early teens, I learned to control it, although I had no clue what it was.

I noticed whenever I took a bath back then and tried to generate this energy; it would start at my head but always stopped wherever the water level met my body. I assumed because water and electricity does not mix that even the spiritual energy would not cross that water barrier.

Today, I have full control of my spiritual energy. I can even generate the energy to flow throughout my body and step into a shower still feeling that energy while water flowed all over my body.

I grew up in Detroit, Michigan, and my mother has always loved the east side of town. Most of my friends lived on the west side; needless to say, I favored that side of town. Unfortunately, I rarely got the chance to get on that side of town until my high school years. My grandmother lived on the west side, and I loved being at her house. I moved into her home in order to go to Chadsey High School which was on the west side of Detroit.

Going to school in those days was pretty uneventful. I was a quiet kid not having or wanting many friends. I went to school, came home, watched TV, ate dinner, and then went to bed. That was my routine, and every blue moon I played baseball and my favorite sport, basketball, with the neighborhood kids, but I always came straight home soon after playing.

There were very few friends whom I enjoyed playing with, but there were also many I just *knew* were bad news who seemed to live for trouble. Worried about her favorite grandson, my grandmother sat me down and asked why I never hung out with the other kids in the neighborhood. I guess that was her way of asking me if I had any social issues. LOL.

I explained to my grandmother that some people just didn't *feel* right to me, and if they didn't feel right to me I just *knew* not to hang around them. In trusting my intuition, I escaped the serious trouble many of those kids ended up in. Maybe it was my guardian angels watching over me. It could have easily been my psychic guides. It could have been God watching over me. Either way, I was very Blessed growing up.

I was never hospitalized. I never spent any time in jail or got into any major trouble. NOT to say I was Saint Mark or anything. LOL. As a toddler, everyone in the neighborhood used to call me Damien (the OMEN child), because I was so bad growing up. I mean everything from hitting people and neighbors with water balloons when they were on their way to church on Sunday mornings to fighting and cursing like a sailor since my first words.

In my mother's social circle, there was a joke going around that she took me somewhere and switched me out with another child when I was around six years old. For some reason, I did a complete 180 degree change and became this calm mild-mannered soft-spoken child as opposed to the terrible little toddler I was. I believe everything happens for a reason, and it was simply my time to change and finish growing into who I am today.

CHAPTER THREE: *déjà vu*

Haiku:
Something makes me feel as if I've been here
before, it's a gift I have

For several years growing up, I went through many phases of déjà vu. It was stressful and a bit scary for me. I would often feel as if I had conversations before I had the conversations. The feeling was amplified by ten. It bothered me that no one else experienced what I was going through.

I remember vividly an incident while relaxing on my grandparent's porch. I was with Ulysses Walsh, the man I call Daddy, who married my grandmother, Natha after she dated my grandfather, Charles Howell. Daddy was so cool that he did not like being called granddaddy. Whenever I would call him granddaddy, he would squint his eyes at me demanding I called him Daddy instead. This set well with me. I am three years younger than my aunt, Misty, so calling him Daddy did not bother me one bit. Also during this time I did not know my real daddy so I was eager to call someone daddy. I loved him like he was my father too.

Off topic again, but on this one sunny summer afternoon, with Daddy drinking his favorite drink, Blatz beer, and me, drinking my favorite drink, Coca-Cola, my God sister, Niecy, came walking down the street going towards her house next door to ours. It was rather quiet, and the wind was light. I remember first thinking it, then saying aloud that she was going to trip and fall into the bushes in front of our house.

I was merely repeating what I felt already occurred because that was how those feelings were for me. Daddy was not pleased.

"Now boy why would you go and say something like that?"

"Don't you remember this happened already, Daddy?"

Lo and behold, while Daddy had a look of complete disapproval on his face, sure enough, as Niecy got in front of our house, she spoke and smiled but was having trouble walking in her flip-flops. She stumbled right into the bushes in front of our house. After making sure she was not harmed, Daddy and I laughed. Bewildered and amazed, he asked me how I knew it would happen. Feeling a little uncomfortable about no one understanding my déjà vu, I lied saying it was a lucky guess.

Before the days of caller ID, I went through a phase of knowing who was calling before the phone was answered. I would also know who was at the door before the doorbell rang. I'll explain further in the next chapter, "daddy".

Incidents like these would happen more often as I aged. I grew up fearing people would think I was insane if they knew these were not random guesses. After doing some research, I learned that experiencing a lot of déjà vu was an early sign of being clairvoyant.

CHAPTER FOUR: *daddy*

Haiku:
You help to raise me
Always a listening ear
Granddad, my daddy
~Soltreu

Daddy was very important to me. I looked up to him and loved him dearly. Ulysses Walsh raised me as if I was his blood, and I will forever be grateful to him.

The night that he died changed me and put me on the course to my clairvoyant self-discovery. I remember it being very cold outside. Daddy found out months prior that he had lung cancer and was given only three weeks to live. Daddy, being a man of great strength, lived beyond the doctor's prognosis. He seemed pretty healthy considering, until some months later. Daddy had to go into the hospital.

My grandmother moved into the hospital room with him. She wanted him to feel as comfortable as possible, spending her last moments with her husband. I was seventeen, so I was old enough to maintain our home without a chaperone. The night Daddy passed, I was unable to sleep. I remember feeling like something wasn't right that evening. It was very cold outside for that time of year.

I slept downstairs on the living room couch to be in the center of the house. Around one thirty in the morning, the house phone rung, but there was a dial tone once I answered. I assumed someone was playing on the telephone. This happened twice and was before the days of caller ID and the automatic call back option, *69. I was furious not knowing who was playing on the telephone so late in the night.

It was difficult to fall back to sleep. Once I did, the front door bell beeped jarring me out of my sleep. I jumped up, went to the front door, looked outside, and asked who it was several times, but no one responded. Again, I figured someone was playing with me knowing I was home alone.

After finding the closest baseball bat and the biggest knife from the kitchen, I tried returning to sleep while listening for the telephone and doorbell.

When the phone rung for the final time, I let the answering machine pick up and heard my grandmother's tired and weary voice, "*Markey your Daddy just passed.*"

    My eyes almost popped out of my head. I immediately jumped off of the couch and ran to the phone hoping to catch her before she hung up. No luck. In shock, I felt helpless. Through my sadness, I checked the front door one final time wishing I was asleep and this was just a horrible nightmare.

    As I glanced at Daddy's favorite chair to relax and watch television, I felt a presence. I stood in front of his chair and cried for what felt like hours.

I later learned that directly across the street, one of my aunt's was in bed with her husband and noticed that at the exact time I missed my grandmothers call, their daughter, my three month old cousin, Porscha, was standing at the end of her crib reaching up into the air as if she was about to be picked up mumbling in baby gibberish, "*I want to go.*" She had a temper tantrum after realizing she could not go with who I believe was Daddy's spirit.

Funny thing is I don't remember anything else about that night. I don't remember much else about the next day or so other than trying to sleep and help my grandmother get the house ready for everyone who would surely be coming over to pay their respects.

What I do remember is the house phone ringing endlessly for the next two to three weeks. I lost count of the many times our doorbell rang. It was during this time that I would announce who was calling before anyone answered the phone. My grandmother and mom were intrigued, and as the day progressed and the calls continued, they would look to me for answers of who was calling. It turned into a pleasant game. Anything to interrupt the sadness of Daddy's death helped with our mourning a little. The game quickly extended into who was ringing the doorbell.

After his death, Daddy visited me several times. I remember the very first time. I felt him when

I was home by myself cooking, making a meatloaf, as a matter of fact.

I love food and can talk endlessly about food, so let me not get started LOL. I was in the kitchen checking on the meatloaf. I was trying to decide if I was going to have red ketchup gravy or brown onion gravy with the meatloaf, when all of a sudden, I felt a presence standing right behind me. I was in no fear but felt comforted. My first reaction was that Daddy was with me. It instantly made me very emotional. I started crying as if he had just died. Later I learned about that particular emotion being called clairsentient, the gift of picking up on other people's emotions or feelings.

During those days, I had no control over it as I do now. I could not physically see him with my eyes, but I felt a shadow of his extremely tall stature. I was able to tell where he stood as if a memory invaded my mind. That is how this gift works. You receive the images in your mind as a memory and once you describe that image in your head, you realize it matches up with the person you're talking with.

At the time, I could share this with nobody except for my grandmother. Once I shared the information with her, she smiled and said she thought it was very nice that Daddy came to visit.

Not long after Daddy's funeral, his daughter, Cynthia, got married. Our entire family was in attendance, of course. My aunt, Wanra, was running late, *as usual*, for the wedding and asked us to save her a seat in our row. Minutes before the wedding started, I felt a sudden rush of sadness. This sadness was reminiscent of the day Daddy passed and the day he came to visit me in the kitchen. Overcome with emotion, I started crying and instantly felt Daddy around me.

His presence felt as if we were having a conversation in my mind. My being a chatterbox, I started saying things like, "*I miss you, and I love you.*" As I sat with the family, Daddy was ushering me to tell the family he said hello and that he loved us. As I started to complain about Wanra's usual lateness and how I would tell her that he said hello, but she was not there yet, Daddy replied, "*Yes she is. She's sitting eight rows behind you to your left.*"

While I was still emotional and talking with Daddy in my mind, the tissue was handed to me from everywhere. When I was able, I explained to my grandmother what was happening telling her what I was feeling. After telling the family where Daddy said Wanra was sitting, and with puzzled looks, we all stood to look for Wanra. Lo and behold, her and her family was sitting exactly where Daddy told me she was sitting waving to us. I could feel my mother and grandmother both staring at me with that classic *what the f...* look on their faces.

As I said before, he came to me several times for two years after he passed. I could always tell when he was there, because I would feel that emotion of sadness I felt at Cynthia's wedding. During our conversation, I expressed feeling his presence and loving to hear from him but confessed to not wanting the sadness that accompanied his visits.

"They" always say be careful what you wish for, because after my confession, I didn't feel Daddy's visits or presence again for 8 or 9 years. I believe that I had to take some time to learn how to receive his messages without the sad feelings.

When I did feel him come around again, I was excited and also understood how my gift was starting to develop. Since then and even now, whenever I connect with those no longer living, I receive images of their physical appearance in my mind. It helps to describe and talk about them, which makes it easier than feeling the sadness I felt whenever Daddy would visit.

CHAPTER FIVE: *family gifts*

Tanka Poetry:
Many gifts run deep
Blessings are a plentiful
*My family **is***
My family has power
GOD has uniquely Blessed us

Now there are many different gifts in the world. I believe everyone has at least one of them; it's just a matter of knowing how to access and use them. Some people consider their gift a curse. For example, I have a sister who would dream about someone's funeral literally seven days before they passed.

I've always been told growing up that my aunt, Misty, has an extreme sense of smell. She could smell what type of detergent you used in your clothes, or if you had a cold, because she could smell the phlegm in your breath from across the room.

In my adult life, I've learned that my grandmother, Natha, has a gift of interpreting dreams. My mother, Michelle, and my aunt, Wanra, can also feel when Daddy is around them, which makes me wonder where this gift came from in our family. When I learned about the Cherokee Indians in our family, I thought maybe that's where our family gifts came from. Either way, I am always thanking God for our gifts.

My grandmother informed me one day that my aunt, Wanra, and I both had the gift of communicating with people who had crossed over. I was shocked and surprised she had never mentioned it before. Wanra could have helped me early on, had I known she was supernaturally gifted as well. I later learned that my aunt, Wanra, had a different gift than I.

My gifts come to me as images, which is called being clairvoyant, but Wanra received her messages through her hearing memory, as if she's heard them before. She also physically hears them which are clairaudience.

According to my grandmother, the difference between my aunt and I is Wanra was afraid of her gift, but I never was. I also remember never being scared of anything except spiders, *I hate spiders!* I also dislike scary movies. I don't see the point in spending money to have someone try to scare the crap out of you.

Once I took classes learning how to expand my gifts, I was able to see gifts in others. I thought it was strange at first. Whenever I met people and shook their hands, I could tell if they were a good person or someone I should stay away from.

My grandmother has a very good friend, Dee Dee, who possesses some of the gifts I have as well. More often than not, I would go to my grandmother for her to interpret my dreams. The morning following her interpretation, my grandmother would inform me that Dee Dee had the same dreams. It was always funny to hear my grandmother say, "*Dee Dee just called me saying the same thing,*" LOL!

    With most people they never know if they actually have a gift or if something were mere coincidence. It took me to reach my late 30s to realize that I actually had a gift after many many years of feeling kind of weird or thinking that some things were just strange, and also thinking I had a very imaginative imagination. With "Reiki, and Chakra" and ALL the other things out there that people use, I feel like I'm about 50% into my gifts and that there is still much more to learn.

SEARCHING

Something in me refuses to let me

Give up on my inner abilities

Before I totally understood my Blessings

I thought I was going crazy

No one else could see the things

That was shown so clearly to me

I lived a life filled with much déjà vu

I just knew I was losing my mind

Then I discovered myself

On a road to forever

And was shown all the things

I am capable of doing

Something in me refuses to ignore

The positive nagging energy

Created in me known as my intuition

This ability helps many people

Find their own way

~Soltreu

CHAPTER SIX:
Okay, what's going on, here?

Words of Wisdom:
Sometimes, we push things away and question them when we do not understand them. GOD taps on our internal shoulders until we stop running from the truth HE tries to give us
~Soltreu

Now comes the part where I must talk about my *very* best friend, Keith Nelson. When I moved to Georgia at the age of 24, I had a few clairvoyant experiences but did not know what it was or how to use it at the time. Through my roommate, at the time, I met a very good friend who had recently moved to Georgia from Baltimore named Keith Nelson.

Keith was the type of person who had friends all over the world. I had never seen so many people call him their best friend, which shocked me, because I felt like I was his best friend. The one common thing that I always heard about Keith was that he had this gift of bringing people closer to God and showing them who GOD was and what GOD meant to him. But to me, Keith was a hilarious, funny, smart, and down to earth. The best friend anyone could ask for.

I used to love hearing his loudmouth come into my house. (He always found a way in). I could be upstairs sleep or watching TV when I would hear, "**MARCUS HOWELL**!!!! What are you doing? I'm hungry, let's go to a show. Come go to church with me!" LOL. I can't help but to laugh every time I think about him and it was because of him that I started going back to church.

Usually on Sunday mornings, I would stay in the bed and watch TV or see which NBA game was coming on that day. Like clockwork 10:15 every Sunday morning, (because he was always late for everything) Keith would come into my house screaming my name and asking me to get up and go to church with him. If I was sleepy and told him no, he would raid my closet and pick out an outfit to iron as he shoved me into the bathroom to get dressed. In other words, I was going to church with him regardless. LOL.

I remember telling him one day that I thought I had a gift and that I could communicate with people on the other side. He kind of looked at me funny, and said, *"Really? Well I want to ask you a question about my dad?* He told me that his father always did something while he took a shower every morning and asked me what it was? Having no clue what in the world he was talking about, I started to guess without knowing how to turn the gift on in order to properly received the message. I always laugh remembering him saying, *"You don't have no gift Marcus Howell."* This was around the same time; I started to doubt it myself.

Keith was murdered a couple years after. This really hit home for me. I remember my friends trying to contact me to see if I was okay and me not wanting to talk to anyone. I felt helpless, because when he passed, I felt like I could've gone to his apartment and get some kind of connection with him to try to help solve his murder. This is why I would love to use my gift to help with unsolved murders.

I did not quite know how to use this gift to help at that time, but God worked things out, and Keith's murderer was caught and sentenced to prison. I remember trying so hard to connect with Keith that I used to give myself headaches and nosebleeds. I kept feeling that Keith did not want to be bothered or disturbed, like he had this wonderful feeling of being so happy where he was that he didn't want me to continue trying to connect with him.

So I stopped trying. It was not until his candlelight vigil at Piedmont Park, I suddenly felt Keith standing in the center of the circle made by all of his loved ones. I could even see in my mind the outfit Keith was wearing. He was looking around smiling at all of us who came out to pay our respects. Holding a friend's hand, I told her, "*Our buddy just showed up.*" Right after making that statement, a strong gust of wind came up over the hill nearly blowing everyone's candles out. I could feel Keith laughing out loud looking at me saying, "*I did that Marcus Howell!*"

That was the closure I needed; it made me feel great, and I also stopped trying to connect with him because I knew that he was happy. Now here we are many years later and I still think about him quite often, and I have had opportunities to speak with psychics and other gifted folks and they all basically said the same thing I been feeling. They were not able to connect with him. This further confirmed that Keith is well, happy, and having too great of a good time singing and talking at the top of his lungs in Heaven to be bothered with us on Earth.

What works best for me is to think of my childhood when the younger siblings would have to go to bed earlier than the older siblings. The comfort came in knowing that the siblings would see each other again in the morning. I see Keith as my brother who has turned into bed early and I WILL see him in the morning!

After over a year of researching and learning what clairvoyant was after meeting JJ in Detroit, a good friend of mine helped me back on my path to being clairvoyant. It all started with a party.

One of my best friends, Antavius, invited me to his murder mystery party. Everyone was dressed in character and had lines they memorized. Towards the end of the night as people were starting to leave, I remained having a few drinks. You'll learn in

Chapter 9, why that usually is not a good idea for someone who is clairvoyant.

I remember facing the television, when all of a sudden, I felt this presence of an older male standing outside on the patio. Although the blinds were closed and no one was supposed to be on the patio, I could feel the presence clear as day.

I asked Antavius who the man was on his patio. He stared at me puzzled before alarm set in. Thinking a stranger or burglar was on his property; Antavius turned on the outside lights, opened his blinds, and physically searched his patio and backyard finding no one. After the fight or flight adrenaline left Antavius, he questioned the authenticity of my "vision".

Being buzzed from drinking, I was relaxed enough not to be concerned my friend would find me insane. I told him I could feel the presence of an older black male standing on his back patio. He was so fair skin; he could pass for a white man. I could also smell a cigar burning, which I later learned was the gift of clairgustance.

In my mind, I received those images, but Antavius just stared at me in bewilderment. He responded by asking the man's name. Moments later, I received an image of my cousin, Chuck, which led me to speak his name in my mind. Just like it happened between Daddy and me, I felt as if I was having a conversation with this presence. For

Antavius' sake, I repeated what the presence who later told me his name was Charles had to say. Known by Chuck, Charles preferred his first name. He mentioned feeling as if Antavius' house was also his home.

As I was preparing to leave, Antavius got on his computer to confirm or disprove my story. Apparently, a former homeowner's name was Charles and fit my description of him. Charles favored the patio along with the basement and smoked cigars.

Being an attorney, Antavius is extremely inquisitive and wanted to know how I knew these things. I was surprised myself because this experience was my first in receiving such vivid images through my mind. It made me say, "*Okay, what's going on here?*"

I kept this experience to myself not even telling my girlfriend or other loved ones. A few weeks later in a conversation with Antavius, he said he wanted to test me and I figured "sure why not" I was curious to see if I could do that again. He gave me some people's first names asking for the first thing that came to my mind. I relayed the name to my intuition and received images of who they were. As I gave vivid descriptions of this person, Antavius exclaimed, "*Man, you really do have a* gift!"

Several days later, Antavius wanted to communicate with his best friend who passed some years ago. Reluctantly, I agreed but was nervous because I had not done any readings at that point in my life.

We agreed to meet at a Taco Bell across town. I immediately saw red flowers when I got in the car for the meeting. I called Antavius and requested he stop by a florist and get red roses for the meeting. Upon my arrival at Taco Bell, Antavius asked me to ride with him somewhere related to his best friend. He drove to a cemetery I had never been to before, took me to her grave site, and asked, "*Okay, what do you get?*" My honest response to him was "*I don't get shit.*"

Of course, I had to explain why I felt nothing. Although her body was buried there, his best friend's spirit was nowhere near that cemetery, so I tried a different approach. I prompted Antavius to put the flowers on her grave, so I could meditate in hopes of making a connection. EUREKA! Connection was made, and I could relay to Antavius the messages she gave me.

    Through this session, I felt it really gave him a lot of closure. I could see his facial expressions change once I mentioned certain things that rang within his memory. As he asked me a few questions, and I relayed them to his best friend, I became a medium to their conversation. A medium is someone who communicates with the non-living.

I mentioned a friend of theirs describing her and also shared some things about what Antavius' friend was going through at a certain time in her life. I kept seeing the woman from the cemetery in a red sweater, which was weird to him, because he said her favorite color was purple. I felt this would make sense later.

Days passed before I heard from Antavius again. He was excited about something he wanted me to check out on Facebook. Once I was able to get on Facebook, I saw a picture he found of his beloved best friend wearing a red sweater and smiling with a look like, *See, I told you!* The picture also included their mutual friend with whom he had since contacted after years of no contact. Antavius told the mutual friend about our trip to the cemetery. She cried and felt the message was meant for her at JUST that time.

Upon seeing the picture, I felt that sadness I'd feel when Daddy would visit, which by this time was just a little lump in my throat and not the sadness I initially felt.

This was my confirmation that I really communicated with his best friend, and also I really need to explore this gift and use it to help others, which leads me into the next chapter!

HE'S GIFTED ME

It hits me
Like a ton of bricks
This energy comes off me
And I feel in the midst
Of GOD's plans

HE uses me
To do HIS earthly healing
Revealing unforeseen truths
I praise HIM while obeying
Reviling in HIS Faith in me

HE gives me undying love
I love HIM because HE is love
HIS love melts all doubts
That my gifts are not mythical
HE's the creator of everything mystical

The Father, Son, and Holy Spirit
Flows through me like a vibrational flame
No one can unlit it
HE called my name
I answered by following HIS Will

It hits me
Like a ton of bricks
Like falling off a cliff and surviving
This energy HE's placed inside of me
Confirms that my gifts are real

~Soltreu

CHAPTER SEVEN:
"psychic" class?

Haiku:
A man who could see
Beyond where our eyes could see
Sees our lives clearly
~Soltreu

I mentioned earlier strongly disliking the word, psychic, so when I came across this online class, I was hesitant and did not want to participate in it. As fate would have it, this class was one of the best things I experienced in my life. I am proud of myself for stepping out on Faith to take the class.

Before I found the right class for me, I decided to go to a bookstore to try to find books about the development of gifts. I wanted to further educate myself on what I was getting into. With the support of many of my friends to follow my dreams, I learned about online classes that cost $200 to $600. Ridiculous and a rip-off!

    I decided to take another trip to the bookstore here in the Atlanta area called *Phoenix and Dragon* to enlist help from an employee. After inquiring about books that dealt with developing gifts in the spiritual realm like clairvoyance, I was led to a section of books where I blindly chose three books. I had one book in my left hand, one in the middle, and one book in my right hand reading from them all for the right one to come home with me. The book in my left hand won. As I stared at this tiny book, I thought to myself, *I need to read this.* The

<u>Key</u> by Echo Bodine was the winning book. It was perfect for me. Short and small, not as thick as a novel and included a CD with meditation techniques was right up my reading alley!

I was accustomed to meditating thanks to my practicing Martial Arts, but I was not a huge fan of reading although my mother and grandmother are avid readers. They could read thick novels in a few hours. I liked reading but never developed that love for it like them.

This book was such an easy read, and I learned so much from it. I especially enjoyed the way Bodine explained things and how she tied things into the Bible making this gift a lot more comforting for me.

It was after reading this book that one of my friends mentioned that Echo was part of an online psychic development class with another young lady named Leigh Hopkins. My thoughts changed to *"Well, maybe this might be a good class to take online?" Viva Institute* was the name of the class and I was excited to work with Echo and Leigh to learn what was going on with me.

After getting over the word, psychic, and not allowing it to deter me from my journey, another possible deterrence appeared. I was too nervous to sign up for the class. It took my friends' pushing and signing me up telling me when I would start.

I got my fears in check and dove into the class excited to see what I would learn. This was a wonderful experience for me. The course lasted for six weeks. Once I completed level 1 of the class, I signed up for the next class, level 2. I was more excited than a child going to school for the first time. I was excited about meeting people, playing games, and having a great time while learning about my gift. I probably drove the instructor, Leigh, crazy. It felt like I had a million questions and needed them all answered! She calmed me down saying things like, *"We will discuss that next week,"* and *"that's coming up soon."*

I must admit that the set-up of the class was perfect for impatient people like me, yet it gave us an opportunity to introduce ourselves, tell our own stories, and to interact with each other. I also loved that we could contact Leigh when and if we needed extra guidance. It was a WONDERFUL experience and I'm MORE than happy with my outcome from the class AND the friendship I developed with Leigh after the class.

In the Level II class, as well as in the book by Echo Bodine, I learned the true definition of all the gifts. There are four basic gifts that someone can possess, which are.....

Clairvoyant means _clear vision_ in French. It describes a person that can receive information through a sixth sense. It also means receiving images and pictures through the mind, your third eye.

Clairaudience means that a person can have the gift of hearing things inaudible to other people. A message may come to you as if you heard it before. You could also physically hear what others cannot hear.

Clairgustance translates as the gift of smell. This means you smell things that other people cannot smell like the cigar smell I sensed at Antavius' house.

Clairsentience means that you pick up on other people's emotions and feelings. Many are clairsentience but don't know it, especially women.

Because so many women are clairsentience, it's mistaken as women's intuition often.

From these basic four gifts a person can be many different things, for example a "medium" has the ability to communicate with people who are dead, or as I like to say on the other side, however it's through one of these four gifts that they have the ability to do that.

I do believe I have all four gifts; the strongest being clairvoyant. Clairgustance is one of those gifts that you either have it or you don't; there is no 50% when it comes to that gift. I never got into Tarot card readings or reading palms and stuff like that. It too much reminded me of the word psychic and of something more entertaining rather than REALLY helping people. Then I recently learned that Tarot card reading really helps the person to connect to other people through you, so maybe one day I will check it out. Keeping an open mind is what I would like for others to do, I might as well start with myself.

CHAPTER EIGHT: *professor x*

"We have it in us to be better men"
~Professor X

My friends make jokes and call me Professor X. I remind them of the X-Men character, Professor Charles Xavier. My being a big kid who loves cartoons and having three X-Men tattoos, this nickname was a perfect fit for me. Although Professor X has abilities that I would really love to have like controlling and reading people's minds and behaviors. I guess being baldheaded is close enough for the comparison so I accept the nickname.

Occasionally I have to slow some of my friends and family down. People can get so caught up in the message and having someone clairvoyant in their lives that they can overdo it. One of my best buds, Orlando, literally drove me ape shit in less than three days, LOL.

It started one morning with him asking me about someone he wanted to date. He wanted me to connect with that person to basically tell him if that was someone that he could marry and be with. Many times, I struggle with being brutally honest with friends. This was one of those times. I got nothing good from this person, but every time I informed Orlando, he ignored me and kept pushing to connect with his love interest.

I was getting upset because I felt as if my gifts were being challenged and completely ignored. This incident required a three way call with Orlando, his love interest and me, which proved to be a HUGE mistake.

I later learned it was extremely unwise to do a reading while their significant other listened in. Its recipe for a disastrous session! Between Orlando looking for ANY ammunition to use for future arguments, and butting in with his own questions, and his love interest behaving like a deaf mute by not confirming the messages I shared, this was a serious lesson learned to never happen again. I'm thinking, "*Woman, are you even breathing*?!"

So needless to say, this later gave me an attitude and I told Orlando that his love interest had the personality of a burnt match! I was getting pissed off feeling like I was pulling strings to do them a favor. The very next morning Orlando wanted me to do a reading with his mom, and then later on the same day, he had more questions about himself and other people in his life. I finally said to him in the nicest way possible that I was putting Orlando on Professor X restriction. He could ask no more questions about anything until I was ready. I never wanted to hurt his feelings or anything. Orlando is like a little brother to me but he's so emotional sometimes I feel like I have to protect him from crazy people and watch him as well, because he's VERY impatient. He understood and agreed.

I like joking around making the, what I call, Professor X pose, which is taking my fingers and putting them on both sides of my head giving a very stern look. It makes all my friends laugh, including me too, but it gets its point across.

One outing at a Mexican restaurant with some friends, I decided to try a specialty drink there. This made for a great Professor X moment. You'll understand why in the next chapter, alcohol. Others joined us, including one young lady I'd never met before. Upon discussing my clairvoyance, she smiled, looked at me, and then said "*You never met me before. Tell me something about myself."* This is usually NEVER a good thing to say to me when I've been drinking, LOL. Without pause, I asked if she had a brother and described him. I followed that up with asking her if he had a young son and described him. I asked if everybody dressed him up like his father. She confirmed everything. I asked if there was some medical issue going on close to someone's left shoulder. She confirmed she had the medical issue.

I tried to tune more into her, and we discussed some medical issues that she was working through. Next, I described her doctor trying to pronounce his name. I knew that it had "ski" at the end of it like a

Polish name. She confirmed his name, and I gave her the good news that he was just the doctor she needed to talk to. I literally asked her if that was enough or if she wanted me to continue, she smiled and said that's plenty. From there I made my classic Professor X pose, and then asked, "*Who's next?*" Which got plenty of laughs.

It's pretty cool that I have a strong love for music and not just any music but pretty much all kinds of music. I could listen to 80s music and go from there to old-school R&B then alternative rock to gospel music. Playing bass guitar and singing really helps with learning new songs and performing them. I also noticed that some melodies and sounds of music give me the same good feeling I get when my energy generates and flows through my body. Something about energy! I just love how it feels. It's like the adrenaline you get from your favorite song, or for me, riding my motorcycle, skydiving or doing anything adventurous. Having a huge imagination as a kid, and even being a big kid today, reminds me why I like being called Professor X.

CHAPTER NINE: *alcohol*

*Words of Wisdom:
In the midst of our confusion, we often reach out to others for what we should pull out from within
~Soltreu*

Now many of my friends who really know me know that I'm pretty good at mixing delicious drinks. My mom used to have get-togethers and barbecues often when I was a kid, and oftentimes, I was her helper. From cleaning up to playing music or sometimes making somebody a drink. Eventually over the years, while I was a kid, I could make a Long Island iced tea or several other different drinks that adults were making in Bartending School. I did not become a drinker until my 20s, and even then it was only on occasion.

When I first learned what alcohol did to a clairvoyant person it was a very funny experience. About two years ago, when I was taking my level two class of psychic development, I remember Leigh mentioning that sometimes people would have a glass of wine before doing a reading to help mentally open up, so that the reading would be easier. She warned not to overindulge because you do not want to become dependent on that glass of wine. Before graduating, as students, we had to do a practice reading. I was very nervous about doing my first reading and the first thing I thought was, "*Well, instead of a glass of wine, I'll make one of my signature drinks,"* which was much stronger than a glass of wine LOL. I noticed a slight difference in the reading compared to my readings today. The major difference was that drinking inebriates you and opens the mind much quicker. It also relaxes your senses so that is easier to receive a lot of messages without struggling to hear or feel, or in my case see the images. The problem was, after that reading, **I Just Could Not Stop**!

For the rest of the day, I was full throttle saying any and everything to anybody for the rest of the day and for the life of me could not shut it off or in my case shut up. The lesson I learned from that was to not mix the two together. Besides, that would also create a whole new controversy with me knowing that this is a gift from God but also needing a drink of alcohol to use it.

To this day, I don't do any readings with alcohol involved, granted, they are much better if I have a glass of something but I never want to be dependent on that glass of whatever. So what I do nowadays is pay attention when I go to parties, be it a birthday, wedding or whatever type of party it is. If there is alcohol involved I do not want to do any readings. As you can imagine in general conversation with someone, once I mention that I'm writing a book, or the clairvoyant subject comes up usually the first thing I hear from someone is "*Can you do a reading on me now?"* I've learned to say, *"We can schedule something for a future date but not now."*

Usually I end up doing a little something to prove myself. It's funny sometimes wanting to tell the world about the gifts and then sometimes feeling like I shouldn't say anything.

CHAPTER TEN: *so much to do*

Haiku:
As if rules are not enough, we put constraints
on ourselves causing stress
~Soltreu

I was at my church one evening doing a rehearsal with the youth and young adult choir, and I had not shared my gifts with anyone there except for my good friend, Daphney. We have mutual friends, and she became like a big sister to me very quickly. With her being a minister, I learned to lean on her a lot for guidance when it came to things I didn't quite understand, like certain stories in the Bible where people had supernatural gifts, were prophet's, and other stories. Since Daphney knew about me being clairvoyant we had many discussions on the subject.

Uh oh, there I go jumping into stories again. I will get back to Daphney in the next chapter, Judging, LOL. Back to that evening in church. During rehearsal, we would always pray before and after rehearsal so our group would gather in a circle holding hands in prayer. One evening I ended up holding hands with Kim, another one of the ministers from the church. I noticed the past couple of months Kim had been wearing a hand brace on her left hand. When we discussed it, she mentioned that she fell and hyperextended her thumb and her thumb was still bothering her for the past couple of months and wearing a brace helped. After we prayed, Kim said, "*You made my thumb hurt squeezing my hand during prayer.*" I noticed that almost every time I prayed, that same energy flows through my body from my head down my arms and everywhere else. It's the same great feeling I get from good music and other adrenaline activities, so I realized I probably squeezed her hand too tightly and feeling badly, I apologized. What happened next was nothing more than amazing. Without thinking, I took Kim's hand, closed my eyes, and started concentrating. I wanted to create that same energy that I use when I do readings, and I was concentrating on sending it into my fingertips. I placed my fingertips around her thumb barely touching it. She assumed I was praying for her, and said *"Oh that's so nice of you. You're praying for me."* After about 10 seconds, Kim's thumb made a loud popping sound like she was cracking her knuckles, and she exclaimed, *"Oh my GOD what are you doing to my thumb?!"* I told her to hold on a second because it was about to pop again. When it popped again, Kim's eyes got big, as I opened my eyes and took my fingers off of her thumb. Daphney was watching the whole time. No longer about to contain her joy, Daphney started jumping up and down excited. Daphney knew what was going on and was excited to witness this miracle take place.

Kim looked at me, moved her thumb around a few times, and then she said, "*You just healed my thumb; I swear all the pain is gone, and my thumb has been bothering me for months!*" She placed her hand brace on her seat and never wore it again. When people asked her about her hand brace, she would tell them, "*Marcus heeled my thumb.*"

This was a confirmation to something that JJ mentioned to me a long time before, saying that not only was I clairvoyant but that she also felt that I was a healer as well. This was something new to me. I never saw myself as a healer, but we usually never know what God is going to do with us. Now that I know how to use this gift, I have used it to heal others, and so far, every single time it has worked. Thank God!

I know that there is much I need to do on this Earth while I'm here. I feel like being clairvoyant along with my many other gifts affords me the ability to not only my family and me but others as well, and I'm perfectly okay with that.

CHAPTER ELEVEN: *judging*

Scripture:
"Do not judge, or you too will be judged"
Matthew 7:1

Please, trust me, the LAST thing I want to do is start a huge debate about this gift. The most drama I get is from hypocritical folks who say things like, "*that's the devil.*" I have personally noticed that since I started using and learning how to develop this gift, that the more often I go to church or develop my personal relationship with God, the stronger this gift becomes, therefore to me, it confirms that this is a gift from God and not the devil.

Back to my friend, Daphney. She has ministered to me that "*ALL gifts are gifts from God,*" and the devil was not in the business of giving out gifts. Funny thing, The only time I had trouble reading someone was on a flight back home to Atlanta from seeing my family in Detroit. There was a young man sitting a seat over from me who noticed that I was reading a book by Chip Coffey, Growing Up Psychic, when he said, "*You read crap like that?*" Of course, the look on my face was of pure shock and a little humor. I responded, "*Why do you think it's crap?*" He replied, "*Psychics? That's just crap I don't believe in that,*" When I told him that I was Clairvoyant he wanted me to read him to see what I got from him. Here's where it got VERY strange for me, normally once I open up to begin I ALWAYS start getting images in my mind or a thought to start the conversation. In THIS case, I KEPT seeing a huge blank black wall of thick glass that I could NOT see through. And no matter what I did I just could not get around that dark glass to read this guy. The ONLY thing I kept getting was a huge cross in my mind along with the feeling that I should NOT try anymore.

After telling him that I saw nothing for him, and it was something that I should not mess with, he gave me the "*That's what I thought face,*" and then I asked him, "*Is your family very religious?*" he said both of his parents were ministers and very active in the church community. *"But you're not religious are you?"* He replied, *"Well, I was seeing if you would pick up that I'm atheist."*

WOW! It all made sense to me totally then. I told him, *"The reason that I cannot read you is because this gift isn't for you. I have a strong belief in God and I KNOW that if not for God I would not have this gift. This simply is not meant for you."*

I was not trying to hurt his feelings. I can only share it how I receive it. Now when it comes to the Bible I am no minister at all and I cannot pop off quotes at the snap of a finger, but I do have Daphney, She is a minister and like a big sister to me who shared some things with me that really confirmed that I AM on the right path. Bible verses like "*I have also spoken by the prophets, And have multiplied visions; I have given symbols through the witness of the prophets. (Hosea 12:10,)*" and others I learned from Daphney and other folks like my Grandmother further confirms that I'm doing what's right. Judging another person without even giving them a second to show you who they really are is a shallow way of living, which is probably why today I never judge a person until I get a chance to know them for myself. Besides, the last time I checked, I remember the only judge was GOD himself. According to scripture, God gives gifts to edify and uplift his people, to encourage his people, and to warn his people.

CHAPTER TWELVE:
everyday clairvoyant

Haiku:
My daily living brings about more healing,
thanks to my GOD,
Jesus
~Soltreu

I often meet people and see certain gifts in them. From the outside looking in, I am aware I do not look as I appear. I'm a Black guy with tattoos who makes pretty good drinks, loves to laugh and have fun, would love to skydive often, rides motorcycles, sings, plays bass guitar, cuts hair, works out, draws, and a few other things as well. But something that you don't see is a person's spirituality.

I tend to see a lot of things outside the box and also see life a lot differently than many other people. The joy that I get from doing some readings with people or healings gives me a lot of completion and makes me feel like I'm here for a very good reason. There are certain situations that come across my path when I cannot help but to try to help someone like once I was out to eat with friends and saw a young lady with a button on her shirt reading RIP. It pulled at my heart, even though she was wearing the biggest smile on her face and looking so happy. In seeing her memorial button, I had to share with her that I was clairvoyant. She sat with me, I could tell she was fighting back tears but the message nonetheless was what she needed to hear. Her friend who passed was okay, and her transition was not painful.

When my baby brother with whom I have shared a very close bond with since he was a baby, Fredrick, was overseas I learned during psychic development class level II that clairaudience is also when you think about a person so often during the day and you continuously say to yourself, "*I need to call them; I need to call them!* And then all of a sudden, your phone rings and that person is calling you! You literally put so much energy and thought into the universe that person has a thought, '*You know I need to call them'* and then calls you, you're spiritually connected.

Back when I was taking my psychic development class, Frederick was overseas in Kuwait for little more than a year, and I just sent him a care package full of all his favorites, cereal, cereal and more cereal along with a bunch of different candy. It dawned on me that I could do some of my exercises for my class with him. Being that he was on the other side of the planet, if he gave me a first name of someone over there, and then I provided a reading for them. There is no way in the world I could possibly know the person so I tried it and said what the heck, he gave me the name of someone that he knew overseas who also lived back home in Michigan. When I sent an email back with a lot of information I got from the person's name including tattoos, a description of her home back in Michigan, her hair, her recent travels, and a few personality traits. This became so much fun to me that I asked for many other names to do this more often. This became a fun game for all my friends to share with me. Since then, I still LOVE that this gift has Blessed me in so many ways that I can only begin to guess where this is going to take me. If nothing more than helping people in any way possible then so be it. I always keep GOD first in all that I do, and with that I know that I can't go wrong. Whether you believe in or even heard of these types of gifts before, there's one thing you have to ask yourself...... "*Why not?*"

I have never been in any situation where I felt afraid. Even though I hate scary movies, TV shows and movies about someone like me is very interesting and exciting to watch. I especially love the TV show, *Celebrity Ghost Stories*. Yes, during the show they do try to scare you and make a scary experience, but the genuine stories of people telling the show, to me are fascinating. And hey, I guess I have a few ghost stories of my own, LOL.

Clairvoyant... My Definition, My Story

EXAMPLE OF AN ACTUAL READING EXPERIENCED BY SOLTREU

As a friend, I have been privy to experience firsthand a few of Marcus' readings. I was able to see for myself how he gets prepared. Mind you, I too have had a session or three with Marcus, which is how I know for myself that he has a beautiful gift. The first reading was a phone reading with Lady X. As Marcus connected with Lady X, they first shared a brief conversation before the reading started. Lady X sounded hopeful and slightly weary but was ready for what was in store for her.

I watched Marcus meditate for a few moments to open up after he informed Lady X to write out three questions. He said when you physically write down your questions, *that you physically put* energy into those questions. Once Marcus was open and ready, I witnessed goose bumps all over his arms, which was further physical proof of what his body goes through when he is connected with his spiritual energy.

Lady X was prompted to ask her first question which was about a serious career move for her. She wanted to expand her business and was unsure if she was headed in the right direction.

After receiving the confirmation she needed, Lady X's mood brightened. Marcus guessed her second question and revisited a prior session between the two where her concern was initially raised.

After expressing issues with her health, Marcus reiterated that he saw the same answer as previously discussed and for her to take the proper steps ASAP. After Marcus answered Lady X's final question, she sounded relieved and surer of the total direction in her life. Most times, people just need confirmation that they should trust their own feelings, but *Some* NEED proper guidance and often an intervention.

After the reading, I watched Marcus meditate to close the transmission. Throughout the reading, I noticed the goose bumps remained. Once closed off, they were gone.

The closing off of the transmission between Marcus and his intuition does not mean he is no longer in touch with his clairvoyance, it only means he closed off from receiving messages about the current session or reading.

EXAMPLE READING SESSION #2

I remember telling my aunt, Wanra, about my being clairvoyant and about my doing readings and studying for the past year to year and a half. I could feel the excitement in her voice and my also feeling that she had a gift as well, I knew this would turn to a lot of future conversations. A couple of days later she asked me if I wanted to do a reading with one of her coworkers, and I said sure, so we set up a reading for one early evening and that's when I met Rebecca.

All I knew about her was that she was a coworker and that's pretty much it. I never spoke with her before so I was a little nervous at first but a firm believer in what I do. I went into it with an open heart and an open mind. I called her, and she answered the phone ready for our session. I started by doing my usual meditation to open up and it seemed like so much information was jumping out at me before finishing the meditation. I quickly asked if her father had crossed over. As she answered yes, I immediately felt the sadness in her buildup like a volcano erupting. It was a very strong love she had for him and the next thing I saw was a vision of her father resembling a Latin man. Next I asked the following questions: *Does he have just a mustache with the caramel skin complexion with short curly hair? And if he was military or a police officer?"*

She confirmed all of these things and started crying to the point where it took concentration for her to speak where I could understand her. I asked if she did a lot of crying and praying alone in a certain room in their house. She told me the only room she could find privacy in was her bathroom where she took long showers for personal time. She kept a necklace that belonged to her father hung on the wall and noticed that every time she was in the bathroom, it moved on its own. I also felt that was her dad coming around to comfort her during her family issues. I saw the word, Charles, in my mind, so I asked her who Charles was and she said "*OH! That's my husband's father who I was very close with as well!*"

This was a good reading for her. I felt great helping her with some closure and answering some questions. Rebecca was comforted to know her father was around her in her time of sorrow.

EXAMPLE READING SESSION #3

I had been best friends with Denene for well over 20 years, and like most of my friends, she had no clue about my gifts. It dawned on me before she came to visit me in Atlanta that I had not shared my gifts with her. She mentioned bringing a friend with her, and this being our first meeting, Denene already knew my request if I was going to do a reading with her friend.

I always ask that people tell me little to nothing about the person that I am doing the reading with. When someone saturates me with most or all of the information about someone, it's difficult to receive any information on them because my brain is too busy processing all the information that I have been given.

With no information given to me, I was anxious about meeting Shalonda. The next afternoon the opportunity presented itself for us all to talk. The four of us were all sitting and having my *Watermelon Mojito's*. Denene, Shalonda, my friend, Lamarr and I were conversing when I felt that it was the time to start my chat with Shalonda. Almost instantly Denene and Lamarr got silent and just listened. I started by telling her that I was writing a book and what the book was about, then stated that I wanted to do a reading with her. Oodles of information poured into me that before I even opened up I had to quickly grab paper and pen to get everything jotted down.

The strongest feeling I received was about her parents having two totally different opinions on religion when It came to her and her siblings. Shalonda confirmed that her father was Muslim and her mother was Christian.

From there I received a mental image of her father; I asked if her father kept a thick beard with huge thick like(DMC from RUN-DMC) glasses, tall with paper sack brown skinned with a quiet but very serious personality. She confirmed, then asked "how did you know that?" LOL, I just love those moments (I LOVE seeing GOD at work). Things then became kind of sad when she wrote down a young man's name that she was close to who had passed on. It turned into a great closer for her to hear the messages he had to pass on to her.

She had to excuse herself for a few minutes, but once she returned I had my back to her and I was attacked by the biggest and nicest hug I could have ever received! It made me feel SO thankful. She mentioned that a HUGE weight had been taken off of her shoulders, and she felt blessed to have had that talk with me. I replied with telling her that it made me feel blessed and honored that we had the talk as well.

THANK YOUs

First I have to say THANK YOU!

To God for being the head of my life. I know and realize that without HIM none of this would be possible.

Next I would love to say thank you to my little sister from another mother, Soltreu, but I call her, my Lil Bit. Trust me, I know and realize that this book would not be possible without you! I feel like God has only JUST begun to Bless you on your journey to success in life. I'm Blessed to have you in my life. Never have I met a writer who is so passionate about writing, I love you and I thank you for everything.

To my many family and friends I love you all!

To my grandmother, Natha Walsh, I love you and thank GOD for you every day. There aren't enough words in the dictionary to tell you how much I appreciate and respect you.

To my mother, Rosa Michelle, I also would not know where to start to thank you for how you Blessed me all my life;

I love you!

My dad and Grandad, James Renfroe Jr and Sr.

My brothers and sisters, Jeffrey Howell, Frederick Howell, Sonya Renfroe, James Renfroe, and Bianca Renfroe. And the many adopted mothers I have grown to love in my life.

Cookie Cook (God Mother), Brenda Collier, and Brenda Renfroe.

To my three aunts, Wanra Pearson, Misty Walton and Tracy Howell. All my cousins in which I have way too many to try to type in one book. And to my friends who are like family to me. Again, way too many to put into one book. I have to say to all of you that I feel so surrounded by love and spending time with all of you means a lot to me. I cannot say thank you enough and I also can't say I love you enough.

And to finish this book off right, I feel like I have to finish this story where I started it, Johnnie Fiori (JJ), I Love you so much for opening my eyes to all of this, and I look forward to our Skype talks and seeing you, I love you, Babe!

If you do not see your name, please, don't take this personally. It is not because I have not thought of you. You all make me a better person. I just had to shout a few folks out, and say thank you!

Special thanks to Sidney Laws Photography and Sidney Laws! I Love you and thank you for everything!

To the best graphics designer ever, Maurice Ingram of ALL-IN-MINDS Designs, thanx a million for my cover!!!

Marcus Howell

A WORD FROM THE AUTHOR, MARCUS HOWELL

I must send an extra special thank you to all of you who trusted me enough to purchase and read my story. I want you to take from it that having gifts that make you feel strange or alone does not make you strange, and you should not feel alone.

To those who bought the book out of curiosity or belief, I hope that you get from my words the authenticity and honesty of my character. I am not trying to change the world...well, maybe I am, but I only hope to help those who need to get in touch with their spiritual side.

If I can help you with closure or life's struggles, then I have done my job. With this gift, I also must learn when to say, NO. I do not want you to depend on the Clairvoyant gift as your only method of living. You have a wonderful skill called Common Sense. You also have intellect, knowledge, and your own sense of intuition to guide you.

Growing up, there were days when I would be off by myself mystified because I thought something was seriously wrong with me. I was too afraid to talk with anyone about my "issues", because I did not want anyone to think I was crazy.

This is why I also wrote the book. I want you, who may have a gift, to know you are not insane.

I want any parent or guardian or anyone who are around children to understand the child and not make them feel crazy with silent stares of confusion like it was for me.

I *am* glad that I am not insane and really do have a gift LOL. The more I learn and grow in my Faith, the stronger my gifts are and the stronger my ability to control my gifts become.

In this next section, I will give a brief tutorial on how to find your gift or gifts. This is not for the faint at heart but for the believer. You must be ready to take control of a certain part of yourself that normally goes untapped. **BUT** it can also be fun, so strap up and get ready to unravel your gift or gifts.

I'll start by saying that I'm about to describe what actually goes through my mind when "opening up" before starting a reading. (caution to those who actually picture things as they are being told, I can be very detailed).

The first thing I do is imagine a light switch on

my forehead just above my right eye. Next to that light switch is a closed eye right in the center of my forehead (third eye).

Your third eye is the 6th sense that helps you receive images when reading someone. I imagine flicking that switch and my third eye opens. (I always see my third eye as a little larger than my eyes and a royal blue in color).

Once my third eye is open, then I imagine a zipper starting at the center of my hairline/forehead that unzips toward the back of my skull.

I unzip it and underneath there is a bright white light coming from within my brain. (It's opening my mind to receive the messages that are about to come through). Then my ears double in size and become psychic ears to receive any messages that may come through them.

Next, I imagine all of the energy that flows through my body as light and electricity. I concentrate all of the light and electricity into a ball the size of a pool cue, then I place it on the back of my neck to give me energy through whatever mental journey I am about to take.

The next transformation is in my solar plexus, the pit, of my chest. I imagine a small white light (inner voice) opening up, and the **LAST** thing is; I imagine roots (like a tree) growing from my legs and lower half of my body growing out of my body and into the ground (grounding me).

WHEW! I know that sounds like a lot to go through before reading someone, but it takes me about 25 seconds to do all that or "open up". It also may sound unreal, but it is real to me.

Finally before I get started, I ask GOD for clarity and for me and my personal self to be moved aside, and that whatever message he wants to pass gets to the right person. And of course, once I'm done I do everything in reverse, and thank GOD for the opportunity and the gift. Last but not least, I ask GOD to clear me of everything so I don't carry any energy from the previous reading.

Man! That Psychic Development class was a great thing for me. I had to be VERY open minded and get over my fear of failing and try the exercises they gave me. Of course, I do not say all this to scare people away. I know that this will not ring well with the very religious, but I MUST say again: *I pray and believe in GOD.*

Keep in mind, I am VERY spiritual, and since I have been doing this and keeping my relationship with GOD; the gift has gotten stronger and stronger every day. And again, as I have learned, **ALL GIFTS COME FROM GOD**.

Every now and then, I can create this energy or charge that happens throughout my body and bypass a full opening up and still receive the message.

Now Ladies!

Have you ever walked into a room of people and all of a sudden got a sick or nervous feeling in the pit of your stomach? These days at work, on the streets, around the house and family, you can be sure that there are plenty of *negative energy* out there. Most people assume that they can't take on other people's negative energy……. YOU CAN!

Whether you realize it or not, it's NOT good for you. Women's intuition can also be Clairsentient. One anecdote of the negative energy is when you start feeling tired or upset for no apparent reason, get some sea salt. Use it in the shower before cleaning up. Sea salt naturally removes negative energy, and I have learned that sea salt showers (or baths) at least a couple times a week are a great stress reliever.

Déjà vu is often a good sign that you may be Clairvoyant; I learned that the hard way, LOL.

Our guardian angels or spirit guides (whatever title you like to give them). They can't just walk up to you, and say "hey! Guess what?!" LOL. However, what they can do is send an image into your mind, or give you a thought or a memory.

This is usually what happens while I'm doing readings. I truly feel that almost everyone has some gift, but being that there are SO many gifts out there, it's hard to know which gifts you may be blessed with. The thing is, *you cannot be afraid of them or feel scared to explore, research your gifts,, and be around like minded people.* **TRUST ME.**

SIGNS

What I want to do in this section is give you some tell-tale signs that you may be "gifted". I will also try to help you find out if you have any of the other gifts.

> Déjà vu, words jumping out of your mouth before you realize what you said, images popping into your head all of a sudden, thoughts coming to you as if you have heard them before, a sensation or feeling coming over you all of a sudden, the room feeling heavy all of a sudden often, feeling a cool breeze when there is no source, sometimes feeling like you're not alone.

These are some things a person may experience that may be their early sign(s) that some gifts may be developing in them.

Honing your gift is an important and major part of having the gift. You must be in tuned with your inner self in order to process the appropriate messages. You will learn how to separate your own prejudices and thoughts from what your gift is trying to show you.

Fear not, this is just a short session to help you get started. Relax, and get ready ...

MEDITATION

Watch out because this meditation is *VERY* relaxing and can make you extremely sleepy. I call this the God room........

First, I find a VERY comfortable position on a cozy sofa or bed. Totally relax your whole body from toes to your eye lids. Imagine a spiral staircase inside the room you are currently in, going up. Visualize getting up from where you are, going up the staircase slowly, and feeling the steps beneath your feet.

Once getting to the top floor, enter a HUGE bright room. Inside this room, you feel very happy and blessed. I call this the GOD room because once

I make it to this room I have my personal conversation with HIM, and the joy that comes from my time there is amazing!

Talk to HIM, and listen to whatever thoughts come to your mind during your time in the GOD room. Don't be surprised if a loved one comes to you who has crossed over while there.

Everyone's GOD room is different. My GOD room has ceilings so tall I cannot see them. There is a huge tree and a large comfortable sofa where we sit and talk. My spirit guides are also there sometimes. I feel that I have two, and both have different reasons for being in my life.

One, I feel helps me with being Clairvoyant, and the other I feel helps me with healing and a lot of my future visions I get.

Try this exercise to connect with God and yourself, along with whatever else is out there; remember to **NEVER BE AFRAID**......

God bless you and Thank you!

Marcus Howell

A WORD FROM SOLTREU

This is a special message TO Marcus. Thank you for listening to GOD as HE leads you into an unfamous path of healing and helping others.

GOD has set out a plan that you are following to HIS enjoyment.

There's something about the name

Sweet Jesus that allows us to follow his lead

We may question our direction

But GOD never leads us astray

Or let's us down

HE's a mighty GOD

I thank you

For all you do

I thank you for Marcus too

I love you, LORD

I thank you for Marcus

~Soltreu~

Made in the USA
Charleston, SC
27 December 2013